Penelope
Be Kind to Animals

E. Brauner-Hughes

Copyright © 2020 E. Brauner-Hughes

All rights reserved. No part of this book may be reproduced or transmitted in any form or by any means, electronic or mechanical, including photocopying, recording or by any information storage and retrieval system, without permission in writing from the publisher.

Any resemblance to persons living or dead, as well as any location, event, or entity is purely coincidental. This book is a work of fiction.

Love-LovePublishing—Madison, WI
Paperback ISBN: 978-1-7334454-6-7
Library of Congress Control Number: 2020930435
Penelope: Be Kind to Animals
Author: E. Brauner-Hughes
Available formats: eBook | Paperback distribution

Background illustrations: Diego Sanchez
Character illustrations: Junior Designs
Editing and art layout: E. Brauner-Hughes

Printed in the USA Love-LovePublishing

Dedicated to all little girls and little boys. You are loved, you are precious, and *you are special*.

Dedicated to all of the little creatures of the world. May we all live together in love and harmony. May we all take care of our planet and each other

I dedicate this book to my husband Byron, my children and grandson, for their endless support.

"Timmy and Christopher have special new family members. Will mom and dad let me have a new family member of my own?"

It was Saturday morning. Mom and dad had planned a wonderful trip to the shore. It was mom and dad's special place. Penelope loved going to the shore. There, she could see boats sailing, birds flying and fish popping in and out of the water. There was lots of grass along the way, sand, and fresh air. Sometimes whales swam very close to the shore. When Penelope saw all of the fish and animals she asked mom and dad if she could have a pet of her own. She imagined a giant tank with lots of fish in her bedroom. Penelope loved fish, especially tiny ones.

"Mommy and Daddy can I have a fish?" Penelope asked.

"Pets need love and care," Daddy said. "I don't think you're ready for a pet of your own."

"Oh please!" Penelope cried. "I promise I will take care of it."

"When you show us you can take care of a pet we will let you have a one. When a family adopts a pet, the pet becomes a member of the family. Animals have feelings and require special care and attention. What if you get bored?" Mommy said.

"Pretty please!" Penelope begged.

"The answer is *no,*" Mommy and Daddy said.

Penelope was very sad and started to cry. The whole day was ruined.

The family went home. Penelope was still very sad until Christopher and Timmy visited with two new friends for Penelope to meet. Timmy and Christopher's mom had adopted two new pets!

"What are their names?" Penelope asked. She was very surprised.

"Sparkles is the black one and Pickles is the white one," the boys answered.

"They are so cute!" Penelope gushed. Then she noticed something very peculiar. The cats were not happy. Christopher pulled Pickles' tail and chased her around the room, giving her a big fright. Timmy tried carrying Sparkles in his arms, but she would not let him pick her up. She scratched and hissed, before running away. Sparkles was very angry. There was lots of confusion and noise, scaring the poor kitties. Timmy and Christopher didn't mean any harm, they were just excited, and wanted to play.

Pickles ran under the table and Sparkles hid under a chair.

Penelope became very angry. "*Stop it!*" she said. "You're scaring them! Cats are very sensitive. They don't like being chased and some cats don't like it when you pick them up."

Penelope sat on the floor next to the table. The cats began to calm down and came out of their hiding places.

"We didn't mean to scare them," Timmy said.

"We just wanted to play," Christopher replied. "Cats aren't very fun," he pouted.

"Cats can be fun if you play with them the right way. If you're gentle, they won't be afraid anymore," Penelope said. "You also have to give them space and pet them from time to time."

Soon, Pickles came out of her hiding place to play with Christopher.

After some time, Sparkles joined Timothy and everyone was happy…except Penelope, who didn't have a kitty or a pet of her own to love. Soon, Mommy came in to tell Christopher and Timmy their mother would be arriving and that it was time to go home.

Christopher and Timmy's mother, Ms. Bean, arrived a short time later. Mommy and Ms. Bean talked about the boys and their new pets. Mommy told Ms. Bean that the cats were frightened and that the boys had chased them around the room but all was settled now, thanks to Penelope. Ms. Bean was very concerned. Mommy assured Ms. Bean that the boys were doing a great job now.

"Maybe cats are not the right pets for the boys. Cats can be very rambunctious or very sensitive. These two little kitties are sensitive and gentle. The boys may be too playful for them," Ms. Bean said.

"They're wonderful boys," Mommy said. "I think they have learned a valuable lesson."

But Ms. Bean still seemed concerned.

Ms. Bean talked to Timmy and Christopher about their cats. The boys were sad.

"We're very sorry, Mom," Timmy said.

"We didn't mean to scare them," Christopher replied.

"Please remember that animals are different from people in many ways, but they also have feelings, just like people. They love, they feel fear, anger, sadness and even happiness. They're not toys but living beings and must be treated with tenderness and care like all living things," Ms. Bean said.

Ms. Beans gave Penelope a hug and said, "Thank you for helping with the cats today."

Penelope felt very proud and was sad when Ms. Bean, the boys, and the cats went home.

After her friends went home, Penelope spent time playing in her room. But she felt lonely. She had no sisters or brothers to play with, like Timothy and Christopher. She did not have a pet to keep her company, and sometimes she grew bored playing with her toys.

Later that day, Daddy knocked on her bedroom door and walked in.

"Penelope, I have a big surprise," Daddy said. "Mommy and I talked it over and decided, you can have a pet. You showed maturity, kindness, and compassion for all of your friends today, human and animal alike. You deserve to have a pet. Ms. Bean decided the boys were too active for cats. So we have agreed to adopt Sparkles and Pickles."

"Thank you Daddy, I'm so happy!" Penelope said. "But what about Timmy and Christopher?" She wondered if they were sad about the cats.

"I have good news. Ms. Bean has adopted new pets. Their new pets love to run, chase, nip, and jump! They are perfect pets for the boys."

Suddenly, in walked Pickles and Sparkles. Penelope was so happy she felt like her heart was bursting with joy. But she gave them some space, a new home would take some getting used to. Over time, the kitties were very happy in their new home. They loved Penelope so much, they even slept in her bed at bedtime. Sometimes Timmy and Christopher came over to play with them, and even brought their new pets along for a visit.

It was a beautiful day to play in the garden.

The End

www.ingramcontent.com/pod-product-compliance
Lightning Source LLC
LaVergne TN
LVHW072113060526
838200LV00061B/4882